Tools for Well-being
by Katarina Gaborova

with photographs by
Vikram Anil Vyawahare

&

Conny Mages

Library and Archives Canada Cataloguing in Publication

Gaborova, Katarina, 1979-, author
    Viva : tools for well-being / Katarina Gaborova ; with
photographs by Vikram Anil Vyawahare & Conny Mages.

Includes bibliographical references.
Issued in print and electronic formats.
ISBN 978-1-927032-37-4 (pbk.).--ISBN 978-1-927032-38-1 (pdf)

       1. Self-actualization (Psychology). 2. Happiness. 3. Immigrants--
Psychology. 4. Emigration and immigration--Psychological aspects.
I. Vyawahare, Vikram Anil, 1991-, photographer
II. Mages, Conny, 1972-, photographer III. Title,.

BF637.S4G32 2015   158.1   C2015-901570-7
                                           C2015-901571-5

Design and editing
Peter Geldart and Danielle Aubrey
Petra Books | petrabooks.ca

Front cover picture: Horses with rhinoceros from the Chauvet-Pont-d'Arc
caves, France, circa 31,000 years ago. (Le panneau des chevaux, Jean
Clottes, Centre National de la préhistoire, Ministère de la culture et de la
communication, France)

Gaborova's portrait credit: Pierre Duboue-Sadron
Mages' portrait credit: Wouter Jaques van Hoogstraten
Vyawahare's portrait credit: Aniket Sayam

Acknowledgments

I wish to thank many people for their support: my partner Maylon Rojer, and my dear friends Ben Bourner, Ricardo Sousta, Jennifer Glease, Dr. Svetozar Droba and Helen Dan for their academic opinions. I am grateful to Dr. Henry Ramdin, Pierre Duboue-Sadron, my sister Zuzana Mazonas, my mum Jana Drobova and the rest of my family for always being there for me. Special thanks to Danielle Aubrey, my editor at Petra Books. Additional thanks to Vikram Vyawahare and Conny Mages for their beautiful photography, and to Lyn Drummond, an inspiring writer. Your valuable support has enabled me to achieve this project. Lastly, but not least, I want to express appreciation to my amazing daughters, Monique and Mia, who have always been patient with me. Lots of love to you all and I thank you from the bottom of my heart.

—KG

V!VA Well-being

Author:

Katarina Gaborova was born and raised in Eastern Europe. The fall of the communist regime during her childhood brought with it her first experiences of profound social change, which helped shape her future. At the age of 19, she moved away from her family and home country. She has since travelled through Europe, Australia, Asia and Africa, with a yearning to experience different cultures, learn new languages and explore life. Katarina trained as a psycho-physiologist and psychologist in Australia, and became a life coach and neuro-linguistic programming practitioner in the Netherlands.

She is particularly interested in how change and unexpected life circumstances can influence people's mental and emotional state. She works extensively with the international community – both adults and children – in her private psychology practice in The Hague. Applying knowledge gleaned from various schools of psychology, combined with life-coaching, she assists people in achieving their goals.

Having always been a fan of motivational videos and inspirational quotes, Katarina was inspired to create this book as a way to motivate people and to bring out their best. By combining Vikram's and Conny's images of the natural world with her own inspirational poetry, she hopes to contribute positively to your life and to help you fulfill your heart's desires.

V!VA Well-being

Photographer:
Vikram Anil Vyawahare is a photo-grapher and software engineer. Wildlife photography has been his passion since childhood.

Nature's creations and related conservation issues inspire his work. All of these experiences led him to further develop his skills in nature photography. Vikram feels that the most rewarding aspect of the work is observing nature's creatures, capturing their intimate moments and sharing them with others—especially those who do not have the privilege to experience wildlife first-hand. He has special interests in herpetology as well as ornithology.

Besides photography, Vikram enjoys trekking and drawing. Considered one of India's top eight young photographers, Vikram presently works with Saevus, a leading photography magazine in India.

Picture credits:
facing page 1,
page iii, 6, 10, 12, 14, 16, 20, 28, 30, 32, 34, 38, 46, 48, 54, 60, 62, 66, 68, 70, 74, 82

Photographer:
Conny Mages was born and raised in the German Democratic Republic, former East Germany. She became interested in design, form, material, colour and light while studying architecture in Germany (Bauhausuniversität Weimar) and the Netherlands (TU Delft).

In 1999 she started working as an architect, designer and product developer for a well-established architectural firm, VYA in the Hague. This helped her further develop her talent for noticing minute details in nature's habitat and her intuitive sense of timing in catching the right moment on camera. Photography has been Conny's passion since childhood. Starting with an old-fashion 'Praktika', she learned to develop her photos in a darkroom. In 2012 she created her own company CONiMAGES, applying both design and photography in her work.

Picture credits:
page 2, 4, 8, 18, 22, 24, 26, 40, 42, 44, 50, 52, 56, 64, 72, 76, 78, 80

V!VA Well-being

Contents

Inner Strength

continued...

Physical Well-being

Relationships

~~~

V!VA Well-being

The origin of this deck of cards

As an expatriate, having been born in Slovakia and now living in the Netherlands, working in the field of psychology has given me the privilege of interacting with people from all over the world. Combining my own personal experiences with discussions at work about the concept of "illusive happiness", I was inspired to create this collection.

Human beings enjoy a wide spectrum of emotions, all of which are important to experience. From these, happiness is perhaps the most sought after, yet is fleeting at best. The quest for happiness has been addressed innumerable times throughout history. More than 7000 publications have covered the topic thus far, about half of which include empirical research. Philosophers, sociologists, psychologists, anthropologists, economists and even physiologists have for centuries investigated what constitutes happiness. However, its definition is still yet to be agreed upon.

Perhaps the only definition that can be provided with any certainty regarding feelings, or more specifically "a sense of happiness", is that it is derived from each individual and with each having their own personal definition of the emotion. It can be as broad as feeling a sense of peace or calmness, or as simple as the awareness of positive emotions that arise when one laughs.

Various techniques are used to assist people in invoking happiness in their lives. In individualist cultures such as the United States and western European countries, self-help books and motivational speeches are some of the tools commonly used. In collectivist cultures such as South American, African, and Eastern countries perhaps the preferences fall more towards various spiritual practices, some of which might include the use of affirmations. Regardless, there is not one universal approach to induce happiness in one's life.

Thus, the idea behind these cards is to provide a simple yet effective way to appeal to people of all ages, genders, and cultural groups. The collection has been designed to address various issues of everyday life so that, if anyone feels life's struggle in a particular area, these cards can inspire by encouraging one to reflect on what is happening and to move on. Such self-awareness can give the courage needed to take new steps towards our goals, or help to set up new aspirations.

It has also been shown that rhyming phrases improve learning ability, memory and cognitive processing as well as impressing individuals on an emotional level. Images affect us in a similar fashion but through visual

Love yourself and you will find
confidence will fill your mind.

Vikram Vyawahare

stimulation rather than linguistic. The collection of cards was made to combine both visual images with rhyming phrases in order to stimulate both the visual and linguistic centres, thus providing greater impact on one's emotions.

Why use images of nature?

Psychological studies have described and shown the benefits of human-animal relationships on one's health and well-being. It was also found that people did not always need to be among animals to achieve these benefits. Simply looking at animals or their images can have a healthy impact on levels of happiness. Introducing elements of nature to our living space can have a positive impact on our cognition, emotion, and stress management. For over 100 years physicians have recommended using animals as an additional treatment for illness, for example, to decrease stress levels and pain intensity, and to improve moods.

Finding and improving personal balance

Many sources have shown that several factors can unbalance the internal state of "happiness". A few important factors that people seem to struggle with will be highlighted, such as the act of blaming external sources, for instance, blaming other people or circumstances for the way we feel. This is not to reduce some of unpleasant life experiences, but rather to understand that everyone has control to some degree over their own feelings. By monitoring our thoughts, one can learn to turn negative thoughts into more positive ones, or at the very least to neutralize the negative ones.

Life always comes in waves, and we can learn to make the most of the sense of delight when we attain its heights. Such uplifting feelings teach us to appreciate what we have and enjoy that specific moment. Having experienced life's ebb and flow we know that there are more than precious moments. Hardship and difficult times are equally important as they contribute to our internal resources and our resilience by adding contrast to the high notes in our lives. We learn about ourselves and our reactions in order to implement and improve coping strategies. By taking responsibility and realizing that, to some degree, we can control our mind-set in the more difficult situations, we are a step closer to increased "happiness".

Other factors that influence how we feel include psychological conditions such as depression, panic attacks, and phobias, since they tend to interfere with our state of "happiness". In such instances, it is important to get support from a mental health care professional who can provide several relevant coping strategies.

Some difficult situations, such as having lost someone close to us or losing our employment which is important for our well-being, may leave us thinking that we will never get back on track. Even though at the time nothing seems to make sense, it is possible to come to understand that certain drastic and unexpected changes can eventually inspire us to a completely different way of thinking. By slowing down and pacing ourselves, such changes force us to look inwards and re-evaluate who we are. For instance, it may suddenly get us in touch with our creative side by placing us on a path that encourages a change of career. Some might even decide to finally open that small art shop of their dreams. Even amongst the most negative circumstances there may be a silver lining allowing one to create a positive force or find a motivating element. As co-founder of the computer company Apple, the late Steve Jobs once said, "You can't connect the dots looking forward; you can only connect them looking backwards. So you have to trust that the dots will somehow connect in your future."

How to even start when we can't yet see the connection between our own dots?

Martin Luther King once said: "If you can't fly then run, if you can't run then walk, if you can't walk then crawl, but whatever you do you have to keep moving forward." The beauty of this quote is that it can almost be applied literally. I often use it as a basic starting point with new clients.

From a holistic viewpoint, our mind and body are closely connected, with each having an impact on the other. If obtaining mental balance is difficult, focusing on physical health is often the simplest starting point, especially in those very difficult life situations. In order to improve physical health one needs a balanced diet, hydration, and aerobic exercise, preferably 3-5 times per week. Since nutrition needs tend to change regularly, a safe indicator would be to listen to one's own body, as each person is unique and needs to determine what works best for their own self.

After caring for the physical body, the mental state might suddenly improve too. However, in order to achieve a more positive internal state of mind, it is crucial to learn to appreciate and love ourselves including our body, character, personality, skills, and mind. Such focus can enable us to see the positive within ourselves, further improving our moods. Establishing a habit of using a positive, uplifting internal monologue rather than criticizing our mistakes can immediately increase the sense of self-esteem and build confidence. Letting go of the habit of comparing ourselves to others strengthens our own uniqueness. Working on eliminating the fear of being judged by people in our environment can provide freedom and a true opportunity to mould ourselves in the way we feel comfortable.

Everyone has experienced being hurt. Such experiences can even induce feelings of hatred or anger towards others (or situations in which we may find ourselves). This in turn can be detrimental to our sense of "happiness". Learning to deal with anger by focusing on forgiveness can be uplifting and therapeutic. Although many people tend to equate forgiving with forgetting, often these two do not go hand-in-hand. Forgiveness is about learning to let go of the negative emotions, releasing them rather than letting them gnaw away at us, creating long-term bitterness. Forgiveness is also about having respect for one's own mind and body and seeking a balanced life.

The following cards were designed to combine the above suggestions which are in the form of rhyming phrases with 40 images of nature. These are accompanied by a short explanation that is related to everyday-life situations. The rhyming phrases can be easily remembered, while the explanations provide simple, practical therapeutic advice. I truly hope that you enjoy this collection of cards and wish you every success on your new path of discovery towards personal growth and happiness.

Vikram Vyawahare

Love yourself and you will find
Confidence will fill your mind.

Love Yourself

It is important to treat ourselves with kindness as we would other people when we feel a lack of self-confidence and have low self-esteem. Putting a stop to our internal critical voice and replacing it by a more compassionate and kind advisor can turn one into a confident person with positive self worth.

You can shift your self-perception by focusing on your strengths. View yourself more positively. Start paying extra attention to your needs and become aware of your own self-neglect and rejection. If there are things that you don't like about yourself, consciously change them by working on your new personal and spiritual development. It is hard work so be patient with yourself. Engage in activities that make you feel honoured and well respected.

Conny Mages

If you rise up after falling
Life's experiences will be worth recalling.

Rise Up

In many instances—"life can be unfair". It is important to realize that even falling is both a part of life and a learning experience. Learning to recover from the down times makes us stronger since it adds to our experiences by making us more adaptable, allowing us to cope and to recover faster from future falls. In some cases, learning from past experience could prevent a fall all together. In this respect toddlers are an inspiration. Regardless of their size, lack of knowledge or maturity, they never seem to give up. They strive to walk and in the process, stumble, fall and hurt themselves. Yet they always get back up and try again, repeating the process over and over until they eventually finally succeed.

What can help you to rise up? Begin by: avoid dwelling on the past. Share your concerns with someone who can help you to process the situation, explore other points of view and open up to different possibilities. Set yourself new but very realistic goals. Remind yourself of your capabilities. Additionally, be willing to receive a hand that is kind enough to help you rise up.

Conny Mages

However much you sink down,
Strengths emerge so you won't drown.

Know Your Strengths

Life's patterns fluctuate. We can slide downwards depending on circumstances and our reactions to change. Hitting "rock bottom" means that we cannot possibly fall any further. We can learn from our previous mistakes, rally our strengths and make the most of it. Many successful and famous people have hit rock bottom, only to demonstrate how to bounce back, and at times to achieve even greater heights. Larry King, for example, declared bankruptcy in 1960 and again in 1978, but was capable of clearing himself of debts a few years later.

If this happens to you, reflect on your past experiences where you faced similar situations. How did you survive? Remind yourself that you have survived. Think of what gives you even that tiniest bit of stability—right here, right now. What actions can you take to bring you peace of mind? Do you have someone close to you on whom you can lean? If this experience becomes too overwhelming, talking to a professional may help you find solutions.

Vikram Vyawahare

Be creative with a blade of grass,
Your vision shapes a home that lasts.

Small Steps

Achieving goals takes foresight. Surprising results eventually appear in life when we value the influence of small things. For instance taking small steps towards inventive ideas become an inspiration towards achieving long-lasting results. As this bird shows us, the entire process of building a home can be achieved by placing one blade of grass at a time. The life we want can also be created by determining what we need.

Create a very clear vision of what you would like to achieve, including as many details as possible. Once you have imagined this in your mind, make a plan of all the actions that you would need to accomplish in order to reach your goals. Simplify the plan into small achievable steps and pursue them one-by-one. Your courage to commit, your persistency and organizational skills will initiate the action phase.

Conny Mages

Acquiring wisdom is essential
To achieving full potential.

Wisdom

Wisdom is obtained by acquiring experience and knowledge; we do not always obtain it entirely by ourselves. Parents, friends or people with more experience than us in particular areas can become a valuable source of knowledge and wisdom. Listening to their stories and learning as much as possible from them can be very beneficial. Life is a long journey of constant learning.

There are several ways you can acquire new knowledge. Be eager to learn. Observe your environment, in which you can learn to compare things and to reason logically. Be open to experiment and be willing to try new challenges and ideas. Gain more information by reading from different resources. Seek out the experts and ask questions related to your particular area of interests. Lastly, when learning something new, practice as many times as is required to gain expertise.

Vikram Vyawahare

As hundreds fly in one direction,
Take the path of your selection.

Your Path

History has shown that human beings tend to follow others and to conform. Yet some of the best ideas, inventions and discoveries have been achieved by original thinkers, despite the fact that they may have been harshly criticized, disqualified or ridiculed. Some of these people include Walt Disney, Anna Wintour, Jerry Seinfeld, Elvis Presley, Thomas Edison, Steve Jobs, Bill Gates, Oprah Winfrey, Albert Einstein and many more.

Find yourself and love yourself. Have the courage to do things differently. Share ideas with others, especially with those who were in a similar situation as they are the ones who will understand and encourage you the most. Don't give up your ideas just because others try to change your mind. Be persistent and pursue your personal goals.

Vikram Vyawahare

What might seem an easy way
May not always fully pay.

Easy Way

Sometimes we find ourselves at the crossroads of life, when we are faced with two or more great opportunities at the same time, such as, university placements, travel to different destinations, or several great job offers. All paths have their challenges, advantages and dis-advantages, and at times we find it difficult to choose which one to pursue. In some instances one choice might even seem easier than the other. So when we make an easier choice, we suddenly may find ourselves facing challenges that we haven't even foreseen! Confusing, isn't it? Considering the choice appeared to be the easier one.

If you really can't choose which path to take, close your eyes and imagine the consequences of all the choices. It can be helpful to look inward at how you feel and take note of your physical responses while thinking of all of the possibilities. Often the path to follow is the most instinctual and is associated with strong internal feelings. Once the choice is made, move forward and deal with the consequences responsibly. There is no need for regrets. While the choice that you made was the one that you wanted at the time, experience gained can support you in your future choices.

Vikram Vyawahare

Don't let your misfortunes defeat you.
Harness your strengths and let them lead you

Resilience

Crisis and misfortune are part of life and can be interpreted negatively or positively. We either *give up*, which will lead to feeling more insecure, or we can choose to adapt to misfortunes, such as physical disabilities, and learn to view them positively and turn them into our strengths. Nature and living organisms recover and compensate for many weaknesses. One of my biggest heroes, Nick Vujicic, has been a great inspiration, demonstrating this concept. He has become an international motivational speaker giving hope to thousands of people around the world despite the absence of his limbs.

You can increase your resilience to misfortune by learning to restructure your life in a new way. Understanding the pain that you are living can show you a different way of problem solving. Consciously draw attention to anything positive in your life. Focus on your creativity, perceive new possibilities and use the resources that you have at your disposal. Moreover, receiving and practicing acts of kindness and empathy help healing by increasing the serotonin levels in the brain which are associated with happiness and well-being.

Vikram Vyawahare

Exceptional dreams are achieved
When climbing higher than believed.

Aim High

By setting more challenging goals for ourselves, we can ascend to higher levels of achievement. We may suddenly find ourselves capable of more robust self-development and healthier growth than we could ever have dreamed possible. The story of Tomas Bata is a great example of this; in 1894 he started a small shoe company along with his siblings in Zlin, former Czechoslovakia. Over the years, Bata's company has eventually progressed from a small shop into a well-known, popular "shoe brand" that operates about 5,000 retail stores in over 90 countries world-wide.

You can aim high by first identifying who you are and knowing what you want. Know your strengths and weaknesses. Learn to turn any of your insecurities into new-found strengths. This can be at least partially done by building a new support network consisting of mentors, supporters, and sponsors.

Conny Mages

Losing your balance, falling down?
Imagine yourself wearing a crown.

Wear a Crown

Imagine that the opportunity for a job interview has been given to you for a position that you consider to be extremely important. Since you are out of your usual comfort zone, you may feel the pressure to perform well.

Playing a "let's-pretend-game" can be helpful in these situations. Let's pretend to imagine yourself as being the most confident person you know. Believing this can really help you become that person. Start by changing your body posture, looking up, walking straight, and holding your shoulders back. Rather than avoiding people, approach them with a friendly smile. By pretending to "wear a crown", you may discover how elated you can feel. Your feelings of confidence will give others the impression that you are strong and resourceful. If you practice often enough – eventually you will also come to feel that way.

Vikram Vvawahare

Seize every opportunity that life poses,
Before a window closes.

Opportunity

Many of us have been reminded of the fragility of human life whenever we are confronted with unexpected illness or death in our surroundings. During these moments, we may start evaluating the many opportunities that came our way. If we have explored them, chances are that they brought us further in life, and we have learnt certain lessons. On the other hand, overlooking opportunities could have resulted in feelings of regret and lingering thoughts of "what could have been, if only I had ...".

Regrets can be divided into three groups: things that you did, but you wish you had not; things that you wish you had done, but you did not; and thirdly, realizing the cost of wasting precious time. Looking back at situations that you regret will produce conflicting emotions; you may feel proud that "at least you have tried" or you may have something to laugh about. It is important to embrace the consequences of your choices and to learn to let go of the 'what if's'. Every day gives new opportunities for you to make your "bucket list" to explore other possibilities.

Conny Mages

Caught in the morass of controlled life?
Moving on reduces strife.

Take Charge

Many people have life-changing "taking charge" stories. As young adults, they move to new cities in search of their identity and their place in the world. Wandering from place-to-place, some eventually choose to live in a foreign country, facing once again a new culture, language, and job hunt. Looking for work is difficult considering professional qualifications, experience and language barriers. Many may feel stuck, as if their professional growth, finances, and happiness are suddenly controlled by other people. Even though some individuals have never owned their own business, they may decide to open up their own establishment. Using their strengths to build a business, grow a professional network, and financially support themselves, they may feel the happiness, pride and freedom that come from self-employment.

A few 'lessons learned' from my own personal experience, similar to above, will assist you to "take charge" and help you to step out from under a position of control. Keep your dreams alive; do not let others destroy them. Understand your weaknesses and turn them into your strengths. Be purposeful in your actions. Be strong, face your fears and keep your mind on the solutions.

Conny Mages

Rather than envy another's luck,
Learn their ways not to be stuck.

Envy

Envy originates from the 'fight or flight' response from animals. It is usually associated with dissatisfaction of our self-image as well as our feelings of shame. Envy distracts us and may prevent us from reaching our goals; we lose focus and feel miserable. If we shift the focus to our needs and listen to our emotions, we can become aware of what it is that we truly desire.

How can this be done? Acknowledge your feeling of envy and try to replace it with compassion. You never truly know how hard the other person had to work for their success, the challenges they faced, and the many sacrifices they had to make. Observe those who have reached similar goals and learn from them how to achieve them. By shifting envy into a positive turning point, you will create room for your own self-improvement and eventually, in your own way, you will reach your goals as well.

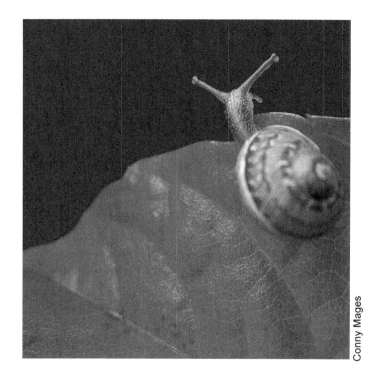

Conny Mages

Do others complain you are too slow?
Keep your pace in order to grow.

Pace Yourself

Many people unwittingly pressure others to take action; for instance, when we say "move on" to those who are experiencing bereavement or grief, or "it has been a year now" pointing out specific timelines, and implying that it is taking them too long to recover. We all cope differently to change or loss, and everyone needs their own amount of time to move forward after overcoming a difficult period in life.

The pace you set for yourself is the correct one. Only you can choose the best time to move on, and that is once you decide you are ready. There are a few strategies that can assist you with the process. Learn to accept the difficult events; face your feelings by expressing them in creative ways (as for example through art, music or sports); and take good care of your physical health. You may also find it beneficial to talk with people who have experienced similar events or you may wish to seek professional advice.

Vikram Vvawahare

Running away never stops pain,
Living through sorrow inspires gain.

Sorrow

Pain gets processed through different forms, stages, and intensity. People develop different coping strategies, for instance, by detaching themselves from the situation, suppressing the event or acting as if it had never happened. On many occasions, not dealing with the pain can accumulate stress. Ignoring pain will eventually cause physical or emotional health difficulties over the years. It is much healthier to deal with painful events as they occur.

Learn healthier and more adaptive strategies to help you avoid old ineffective patterns of behaviour. Strategies that will improve your ability to cope include allowing yourself to feel. This can be done by validating your emotions and realizing that what you feel is completely "normal"; share these emotions with others. Regain strength by taking better care of yourself physically and by letting go of the need to control everything in your environment. Release your stress by means of breathing exercises; visualize how each inhaled breath brings a new positive fresh energy and how your exhaled breath releases the old and negative one. Another strategy that may help you cope is to remove any guilt you may feel by offering an apology or by forgiving yourself.

Vikram Vyawahare

Do not fear , but change,
As you survey the range.

Face Your Fears

How do we face fear? The more we avoid uncomfortable or new situations such as introducing ourselves to new people, or finally calling to ask someone out, the more we condition ourselves to be insecure. Once we embrace our fears as a growth-enhancing challenge, we create new opportunities and develop greater trust in ourselves. It is true that as humans we are scared of novelties, and even more so if we do not know what will follow once we pass into a new stage of life. However, everyone is fearful at some point or another, and we will never be able to completely remove fear from our lives.

Our main goal is to master fear and learn from it, so that it will no longer prevent us from doing what we want. You can begin by getting comfortable with feeling fear. As thoughts enter your mind, allow the positive ones to be more prevalent. Get inspired by other people and their success stories. Darren Hardy (2013) pointed out that all that is needed is 20 seconds of courage to face your fears. "Only 20 seconds" is needed to crush fear by holding your breath, shutting out negative thoughts and simply pushing yourself to act. Once you are able to surmount what once caused you distress, you will realize that you possess inner strength to face your fear.

Vikram Vvawahare

When situations seem dark as night,
Seek a worthwhile shimmer of light.

Hope

It is human nature that our own instinct for survival kicks in during difficult situations. A sense of hopelessness often walks hand-in-hand with the sense of helplessness. We feel both emotions when we have lost control over our lives. However, if we can come to terms with what has made us helpless, this may well help us to regain some of our control back. Sometimes even the smallest ray of light can make all the difference in enabling us to find a starting point required to change our situation. Most importantly, we must never give up, no matter how hard we struggle with the current situation.

Faced with a difficult situation? Here are few suggestions that can assist you to be hopeful in finding a solution. Find the courage to start all over again. If you feel that you have failed in coping with certain situations, you may have developed false beliefs towards your abilities. Recognizing this, focus your mind on past situations and experiences that you positively resolved; remembering your actions may help you to change this incorrect reasoning. Having people around you, especially the ones you love, provides you with the support you may need during this process. Appreciate how your unique characteristics have indeed made your life significant and worthy.

Vikram Vyawahare

Past decisions effectively count
When lessons learned successfully mount.

Lessons Learned

Life sometimes seems to consist of little pieces of a puzzle. One day we come to realize that some pieces fit immediately while others do not. The gift of hindsight will hopefully enable us to see the whole picture and to understand the lessons learned through certain situations, actions and past experiences.

While keeping your focus on the future, you can reflect upon the wisdom you acquired from past lessons. What went right? What went wrong? How could certain situations and solutions be improved or avoided in the future? If you are making new decisions, reflect carefully on values and goals that are important to you, consider alternatives or other influential factors, be aware of the consequences of your decision and take responsibility for your actions.

Vikram Vyawahare

Transfer the anger that you feel
Into action that will heal.

Anger

Anger is one of the most powerful and motivating emotions. Throughout history, we can see how anger against certain institutions, such as the church or public-education system, highly motivated individuals to pursue specific work, for example Galileo Galilei, Albert Einstein and many others. Anger may be perceived as an emotion of helplessness, when in fact it can enable us to move forward and resolve our difficulties. It has also been suggested that anger is an important component of justice and fairness. As Donovan Westhaver (2014) tells us, "without anger we would essentially become a senseless society that acts indiscriminately without much of any purpose".

When anger becomes too strong or overwhelming, release some of its energy from your system through physical activity, such as walking, jogging or playing a sport. The remaining positive energy can then be best used to create and achieve goals, or to take action on new projects.

Conny Maces

Whenever your day echoes with laughter,
Health and joy will follow after.

Laughter

Laughing stimulates our inner smile. Practicing a laugh in the mirror sends a message to the brain, encouraging a happier state of mind. When we smile at people we don't even know, most of them will smile back. This seemingly trivial interaction can in turn lift our and their spirits. Did you know that even fake chuckles can be as beneficial as real ones? If anything, chuckling may trigger real laughter. How does this happen? Laughter stimulates catecholamine (hormones), which releases endorphins. Once they spread throughout our bloodstream, our body automatically feels happier, more relaxed, and less stressed. Laughter increases hopefulness, tolerance to pain, and energy levels, while decreasing anxiety, depression or other mental health difficulties.

Laughter therapy can include watching funny DVDs, reading jokes, or being around people that make us laugh. If you had a recent operation, hugging a pillow allows you to safely laugh! Also take care if you suffer from any physical condition where laughter could cause you more pain.

41

Conny Mages

Feel like curling up in a ball?
Reach to those who help you stand tall.

Stand Tall

From time to time, everyone feels like curling up in a ball or hiding in a corner. During these moments we may lack the ability to deal with certain inhibitions which mask our strengths and our ability to stand tall, such as shyness, embarrassment, insecurity and anxiety. A simple breathing exercise is one of the most powerful techniques that can be used to control such inhibitions. While there are various breathing exercises, their main purpose is to slow down the breathing process and the heart rate, and to reduce other stress-related physiological activities.

Try to inhale deeply, and exhale as much air as possible. For example, counting to six for each inhalation, and exhaling as slowly, is a simple indicator of slower breathing. Changing your body posture by forcing yourself to stand straighter is another way of learning to "stand tall". You can also increase your level of confidence by reaching out to others with whom you feel comfortable, and that in turn will help you battle some of your insecurities.

Conny Manes

Give up things that weigh you down,
Drift carefree and lose your frown.

Letting Go

It can be extremely difficult to let go of habits, ways of thinking, people and relationships that weigh us down. Often, we might become aware of a certain heaviness, intuitively feel it—or others might notice and comment on it. Yet we still push that feeling to the back of our mind, until one day we feel sad or start developing stress-related physical pains (such as back pains, headaches, neck and shoulder pains, etcetera). We are then finally forced to prioritize and place our own well-being first.

As hard as it may appear, clean your environment of things, including people, that weigh you down. Ultimately it can be very liberating, uplifting, and healthy. Some of the factors that need occasional evaluation include your thought patterns, perspectives on life, certain habits you dislike, your job, and unhealthy life style. Other areas of your life that could wear you down are your choice of partners, negative people in your environment, unsupportive friends that hold you back—all of which may cause you to have irrational fears, poor self-perception and self-image.

Vikram Vyawahare

Have the courage to let yourself cry,
Release all tension and then you'll fly.

Courage

In some cultures expressing "negative emotions", such as anger, sadness, or shame, is not acceptable and can be seen as "losing face". However, venting these emotions can help prevent physical ailments that stem from bottling up our feelings. Interestingly enough an international study[1], that included both males and females from over 30 different countries, has concluded that most people experience relief and feel better psychologically after crying.

Rather than crying alone, you can benefit from the experience of a good, healthy cry by involving a close friend or other social support. Healing can occur by crying in a safe place and after the problem has been resolved.

---

[1] Bylsma, Vingerhoets, & Rottenberg, 2008.

Vikram Vyawahare

Being strong, successful and great,
You still need leisure to recuperate.

Life Balance

Burnout is a debilitating condition that can stem from working and worrying too much. The elephant reminds us of the need to listen to our own body. No matter how strong we feel, how successful we are, or even if we think that the work cannot be achieved without our involvement, we still need to find time to recharge.

Have you ever worked hard for a long period of time and became ill as soon as you took a vacation? The illness was a warning from your fatigued body that you had taken on more than you could handle. Balancing work and relaxation is vital to your well-being. Taking good care of yourself is achieved through a healthy balanced diet, scheduling activities or creative hobbies that make you feel good, doing sports to improve your physical health, listening to music, and visiting and laughing with friends and family. Include some of these activities as part of your everyday agenda.

Conny Mages

Reflect on how far you have come.
Reward yourself for all you've done.

Reward Yourself

Sometimes there is a desire to achieve more and more, up to the point where we forget to appreciate our previous accomplishments. It is important to occasionally pause and enjoy our successes. Such reflection can remind us of all that we have achieved and contributes to self-efficacy and confidence. Reflection is also mentally relaxing as it further motivates us to continue with the work that we have initiated.

Create a detailed plan with many small sub-goals that are quickly achievable. Keep your old to-do lists; marking your progress is rewarding, motivating and will increase your desire to get through the future tasks. Recognize your successes and celebrate them regularly by treating yourself with a chosen item from your reward list (for example having a nice dinner out, meeting with a friend, reading a book, etcetera).

Conny Mares

Age is a not an excuse,
Put your knowledge and skills to use.

New Beginnings

Some people think "I wish I was younger, I am too old to start something new" and limit themselves due to their age. There are also many young people who share the same limiting view, thinking "I am too young, and do not have the necessary experience". Viewing age as limiting often reflects societal stereotypes that inhibit us. One's age is not a disability; it is a referential number.

Being older has many advantages: having years of life experiences and a mature way of thinking, being less caring about the perception of others, and having the time to finally do the things that you truly enjoy. Realize that it is possible to try new activities at any age. Trying something for the first time is also a gift of freedom to discover. And if not successful at a first attempt, remember that trying is never about failing; rather, failure is not having done certain activities or things in life at an opportune time, and later feeling regret for the unmet challenge.

Vikram Vyawahare

Keeping your eyes open wide
Reveals answers by your side.

Eyes Wide Open

Someone I know wanted more than anything to study overseas. Although he was admitted to several universities in his home country, he refused a few of them, waiting for his dream to come true. Years passed by and somehow his international opportunities fell through due to finances, family issues and other reasons. One day he realized that, while he was waiting, his high school classmates had graduated from the Universities that he had refused earlier. While focusing straight ahead can generally motivate us to move forward, there is a danger of tunnel vision which can also cause us to lose sight of what is around us.

Pausing every once in a while, stepping back and looking at the big picture can often bring things to your attention that could have been missed otherwise. Opportunities may come in many guises; and it would be unfortunate to ignore opportunities simply because they appear different from what you originally desired.

Learn when the moment's best
To take the time you need to rest.

Rest

Enjoying a healthy life-style includes finding a balance between work and rest. Pushing ourselves without rest can hinder our effectiveness. In fact, resting improves our effectiveness and productivity at work. This has been demonstrated by Dr. Karl Anders Ericsson[2] and his colleagues from Florida State University who suggested that the best productivity comes in 90 minute cycles coupled with regular scheduled breaks in-between. However, what happens when we overdo rest time and become lazy?

To prevent laziness, you must get back to work. It is as simple as that. Plan simple goals and reward yourself upon reaching them. Motivate yourself by remembering the benefits. Make a to-do list, and regularly cross out the tasks once they are completed. Compliment yourself after each task completion. If needed, remove any distractions from your surroundings to reach those milestones.

---

[2] Dr. Karl Anders Ericsson et al, 1993.

V!VA Well-being

Vikram Vvawahare

Earn the trust of others by being sincere,
The truth of your word for all to hear.

Sincerity

Respect and trustworthiness are earned by being honest with oneself and with others. Hiding something, or pretending to be someone we are not, will eventually result in hurting ourselves and the way others perceive us, when the truth inevitably comes to light. Many people consider white lies as harmless, such as giving someone a compliment when we don't really mean it. Some studies[3] show that everyone lies several times per day, even if just to be polite or to avoid arguments. Nevertheless, any type of lie costs our body a lot of effort, stress and anxiety.

Telling a lie increases your level of stress. When you lie, you must figure out what you need to hide, and make your story seem believable. Then you need to put on an excellent performance to make the lie look genuine. And, you need to remember what, when and to whom you told 'certain things'. So, if you think about it, in the end truth and honesty offer many more mental and physical health benefits when compared to dishonesty.

---

[3] De Paulo, Kashy, Kirkendol, Wyer, & Epstein, 1996.

Vikram Vyawahare

Connect yourself to others
Balance your life, enhance another's.

Harmony

It is important to integrate personal independence with a well-balanced social life. "Solitude" provides us with precious space to reflect on our thoughts and actions. Being alone helps to clear our mind; we can think deeply undisturbed, and with better concentration, thus allowing us to work through problems faster and more effectively. On the other hand, a well-balanced social life has been linked to a general improvement of both physical and mental health, due mostly to providing us with a sense of belonging. Others can often offer us valuable feed-back from which we create our own sense of self-worth.

The balance and harmony between time spent alone and time with others are equally important and necessary. Integrate both in your agenda at least several times per week in order to fulfill your numerous needs in life.

Love is more than black and white,
Harmony grows in each other's sight.

Communication

Relationships can be romantic, intimate, professional, or personal. One of life's lessons is to listen to the needs and opinions of others. By listening to others, we extend our view beyond our own personal limitations. Likewise, expressing our own point of view is also crucial as many relationship problems stem from lack of authentic communication that can lead to misunderstandings.

Help remove these obstacles through open and honest communication in all your relationships. Open conversation will avoid making assumptions of each other's needs. You can open-up to friends by talking about things that are not easily shared with everybody. By listening, and also by being attentive to nonverbal signals of others, you will enrich your communication skills.

Vikram Vyawahare

Never take others for granted,
Seeds of affection flourish when planted.

Affection

Relationships are like a two-way street. When we care about someone, we show them how we feel by giving them affection. People have a tendency of being attracted to those having positive "vibes". Dr. Susan Campbell [4] identified five stages of love: the romance stage begins with the natural force of falling "in love"; the power struggle stage occurs when partners start seeing flaws and differences in each other, usually around 3-4 years into the relationship; the stability stage includes the acceptance of the partner's differences as the relationship moves into a deeper, more mature level; the commitment stage causes the partner to be loved just the way he/she is and an acceptance of the shortcomings of the relationship; and lastly, the co-creation or bliss stage is reached when the relationship grows deeper and serves the world in some way, for instance, when the partners create certain projects together.

If you would like your relationship to grow, practice different acts of kindness, and show your appreciation. And by being curious and playful, you can enjoy a more passionate and healthy relationship.

---

[4] Dr. Campbell, 1980.

Vikram Vvawahare

Sometimes silence is enough
When another has it tough.

Silence

Do you know someone close to you who is going through a rough period, and you don't know what to say? At times there are no words that can be said to make them feel any better. Simply being by their side, showing you care, may be all the support that they need.

Although you might think that your support is not enough, you are actually giving a lot more than you know. By simply "being there" you are demonstrating the qualities of true friendship such as caring, loyalty, and trustworthiness, especially if you had previously promised to be present. Your compassionate support shows your generosity, concern and most importantly your desire to see your friend or loved one feel better.

Vikram Vyawahare

Nurturing those with daily needs,
Warms your heart through gentle deeds.

Nurturing

Nurturing others has a positive physiological impact on our body. The act of nurturing is connected with brain changes associated with happiness. It increases our sense of belonging, and decreases feelings of isolation. It improves our confidence, sense of control and optimism, and in general contributes to a more positive society.

You can enrich your own sense of well-being by nurturing others—without setting limits, conditions or expectations. There are many different ways that you can nurture others. You can encourage them by showing them appreciation and support. Offering kindness and honest communication will make it easier for them to speak of their difficulties. Having fun and cheering others will help take their minds off everyday problems and hardships. Providing emotional support and pointing out their strengths will both uplift and increase their confidence. Being compassionate and accepting of their differences reinforces their feeling of being understood.

Conny Manes

Linking positive thoughts to each other,
Gives new ideas to discover.

Positive Thinking

One idea often leads to another. A positive thought is expansive and creative, and by sharing such thoughts with other individuals, new ideas can emerge which can be mutually beneficial. People having a positive outlook, help each other accomplish inventive endeavours.

Inquire about someone else's perspective to broaden your point of view. Play a game of "what-if-there-are-no-limits" as that can create a very detailed vision of how to handle certain situations. This can bring you one step closer to solutions, for example, on how to find specific resources. If you really can't move any further with your thinking, use a "reverse thinking method"; rather than focusing on how to improve the situation, product or idea, think instead of a way to worsen it. Once you reverse your thinking back again and reconsider all the complications, you will find it easier to counter-resolve with new possibilities.

Vikram Vyawahare

While creating alone may limit your view,
Effective teamwork develops you.

Teamwork

An efficient team that shares ideas will not only lessen the workload, but may also provide an effective method of learning for all. Everyone involved in a work project can share and divide the tasks based on their skills and expertise. Generally, teamwork brings better and more innovative results. Team members can progress much faster yet still maintain their own creative space. People practice taking responsibility for their own share of the work as well as learning to be flexible in order to fulfill common goals. Some of the psychological benefits related to teamwork include having a greater sense of belonging, frequent recognition by others and a shared sense of pride.

What skills do you need to be a good team player? Show others that you are reliable, trustworthy, a good communicator, open-minded, and flexible. Be respectful and supportive of others' ideas. And most importantly, having a positive attitude helps to ensure a healthy, pleasant work environment.

A gentle touch will heal your pain,
Letting true love flow again.

Gentle Touch

Human beings have an innate need to be close to others. Touching and hugging have been linked to an increase of the happy "bonding" hormone, Oxytocin. A comforting touch or gentle hug can be a simple act that contributes to another's happiness. Hugs, holding hands, and cuddles-and-snuggles have all been associated with strengthening our immune system and decreasing stress by lowering cortisol levels. These forms of non-verbal communication have also been found to increase our sense of trust and security.

Next time you or someone in your surroundings are feeling down, lonely, afraid, or sick, reach out and offer a gentle touch.

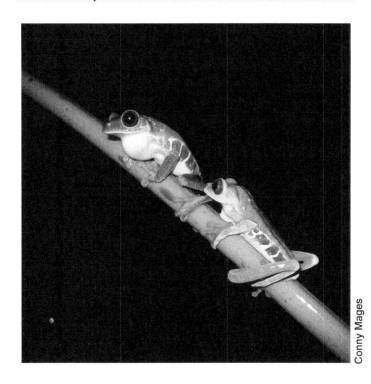

Conny Mages

Your chosen journey seems too rough?
Friendly support helps enough.

Support

Some of the paths we choose turn out to be more difficult than initially expected. Being around gentle individuals who quietly listen, empathize, advise or are simply there for us, can make us feel stronger. Overcoming difficulties becomes easier with caring support.

There are several ways to find support. Talking to someone who can view your situation objectively may help you see more clearly. Receiving a hug or gentle touch from those you love or feel comfortable with can give you emotional strength. Helping others when you feel down can be spiritually uplifting, giving you a feeling that what you do still matters—get involved with a community or volunteer. Caring for a pet provides warm company as well as being a great listener. Keeping yourself occupied with activities that you have always enjoyed, alone or with friends, can help to remove feelings of loneliness.

Conny Manns

Need someone when sad and lost?
Connect to those who don't count the cost.

Connections

Most people who are downhearted tend to isolate themselves from others. They may not want to share their feelings, or may simply have a fear of being misunderstood. At times it is a matter of not wanting to burden others, hoping that by dealing with their hardships alone, they will eventually overcome the pain or sadness. We need to remind ourselves that humans are social creatures, and that we need others the most when we feel despondent.

If you are feeling down, don't wait until someone calls. Initiate a connection with people you feel are comfortable and trustworthy. In most cases they will be happy to listen, to offer you a hand or to provide advice. If you feel uneasy with opening up to others, start in small steps. Find ways to share your experiences, and do not be afraid to ask for a hug.

Vikram Vyawahare

Feeling like you've lost the fight?
Stand up for what is right.

Stand Up

When we find ourselves in critical situations, we may surprise ourselves by the discovery of skills, strengths and abilities we never thought we even possessed. Difficult situations can boost our confidence and teach us that we can overcome any challenge. Most people try to avoid conflict, because it makes them feel uncomfortable and may trigger strong emotions. However, if we don't stand up for what we believe is right, we compromise our own values and morals, as well as depriving ourselves of the opportunities that matter to us. Conflict can be resolved positively, and by showing the other party that we will stand up for ourselves, we earn respect.

Be mindful of what matters and the needs of both parties if you decide to openly face the other person. Determine your expectations and practice expressing them clearly. At a suitable moment, approach the other person calmly and respectfully. If you manage to come to an agreeable conclusion, choose to forgive the other party. Forgiveness avoids rumination or punishment and enables open communication in the future.

Templates

Using these templates
will help you
work towards your
self-established goals.

What helps me stay positive & happy?

- _____

- _____

- _____

- _____

- _____

- _____

- _____

Work/Leisure Balance

Day	Work hours	Leisure Activities Hobbies / Social hours
Mon		
Tue		
Wed		
Thr		
Fri		
Sat		
Sun		

Personal Strengths

- _____

- _____

- _____

- _____

- _____

- _____

- _____

Personal Development

New Goals	Sub Goals
	- - -
	- - -
	- - -
	- - -
	- - -
	- - -
	- - -

What personal achievements
make you proud?

- _____

- _____

- _____

- _____

- _____

- _____

- _____

Rewards
for Personal Achievements

- _____

- _____

- _____

- _____

- _____

- _____

- _____

Physical Health

Day	Monitor Intake		Exercise	Notes
	food	liquid		
Mon				
Tue				
Wed				
Thr				
Fri				
Sat				
Sun				

Personal Bests

Sports	Achievements

Facing your Fears

Make a list of all of your fears:

- _____

- _____

- _____

- _____

Choose one that you would like to overcome, such as a fear of spiders (Arachnophobia).

For example, overcome the fear of spiders by:

1. Feeling comfortable with talking about spiders, and looking at a picture of spiders;

2. Seeing a spider in a pet shop or a zoo;

3. Being comfortable standing close to a spider in your environment.

4. You can make as many steps as you want until you eventually get confident holding one in your hands.

Separate your fear into small steps:
talk about it, examine it and learn about it.

1. _____

2. _____

3. _____

4. _____

*Remember to reward yourself
for every step achieved.*

Some fears can be faced by using the
"20-second-just-do-it" technique.

For example: Take a deep breath, then pick up the
phone and call your favourite person to ask them out.

You may find that your expectations
caused you more fear than the actual event!

Building Self-confidence

Everyone has an internal critical voice.
What does your internal voice say about you?

- _____

- _____

- _____

- _____

- _____

- _____

- _____

Building Self-esteem

Viewing yourself through the eyes of a best friend,
what do you appreciate about yourself?

- _____

- _____

- _____

- _____

- _____

- _____

- _____

Who to call for help

Person	Address
Name Tel Email	
Name Tel Email	
Name Tel Email	
Name Tel Email	
Name Tel Email	
Name Tel Email	
Name Tel Email	

Book Resources

Abreu, P. (2009). The effect of animals on human mood. Retrieved from www.helium.com/items/1307094-the-effect-of-animals-on-human-mood, retrieved on 20.7 2013.

Bok, S. (2012). Happiness studies in ancient Greece? A 2nd century skeptic's challenge. International Journal of Wellbeing, 2(3).

Bylsma, L.M.; Vingerhoets, Ad J. M.; & Rottenberg, J. (2008). When is crying cathartic? An international study. Journal of Social and Clinical Psychology, 27, (10).

Campbell, S. (1980). The Couple's Journey: Intimacy as a Path to Wholeness. Impact pub.

De Paulo, B. M.; Kashy, D. A.; Kirkendol, S. E.; Wyer, M. M.; & Epstein, J. A. (1996). Lying in everyday life. Journal of Personality and Social Psychology, 70(5).

Ericsson, A.K.; Krampe, T. R.; & Tesh-Romer, C. (1993). The role of deliberate practice in the acquisition of expert performance. Psychological Review, 100 (3).

Grinde B., & Grindal Patil G. (2009). Biophilia: Does visual contact with nature impact on health and well being? International Journal of Environmental Research of Public Health, 6(9).

Hardy, D. (2013). www. darrenhardy.success.com/2013/06/20-seconds-of-courage/, retrieved on 19.9 2014.

Johnson, R.A.; Meadows, R.L., Haubner, J.S.; & Sevedge, K. (2008). Animal-assisted activity among patients with cancer: effects on mood, fatigue, self-perceived health, and sense of coherence. Oncol Nurs Forum, 35, (2).

Nepps, P., Stewart, Ch., & Bruckno, S.R. (2011). Animal-assisted therapy: Effects on stress, mood, and pain. The Journal of Lancaster General Hospital, 6. (2).

Schwartz, T. (2013). www.nytimes.com/2013/02/10/opinion/sunday/relax-youll-be-more-productive.html?pagewanted=all, retrieved on 20.9 2014.

Westhaver, D. (2014). www. dondwest.hubpages.com/hub/Virtue-of-Anger, retrieved on 17.9 2014.

Websites

batova-vila.cz

brainpickings.org/2013/04/22/14-ways-to-acquire-knowledge-james-
mangan-1936/

canadianliving.com/relationships/love/how_to_stop_taking_your_par
tner_for_granted_and_appreciate_your_mate_2.php,

effective-mind-control.com/overcoming-envy.html

elitedaily.com/life/motivation/17-things-weigh-youll-give-order-
fly/741269/

emotionalcompetency.com/envy.htm

everydayhealth.com

forbes.com/sites/kathycaprino/2013/05/01/5-critical-steps-to-
birthing-your-big-dream-successfully/

helpguide.org/mental/eq8_conflict_resolution.htm

inc.com/jessica-stillman/5-steps-to-bust-your-envy.html

julietisthesun.com/relationships-2/stages-of-relationship-couples-know/

lifehacker.com/5968613/what-lying-actually-does-to-your-brain-and-
body-every-day

loveatfirstfight.com/relationship-advice/ communication-
skills/decision-making/

mentalhealth.org.uk/ mentalhealth.org.uk/help-information/mental-
health-a-z/A/altruisim/

mindtools.com

planetofsuccess.com/blog/2010/ways-to-fight-and-overcome-laziness/

psychcentral.com

psychologytoday.com

science.howstuffworks.com/life/laughter-therapy4.htm

slate.com

smallbusiness.chron.com/benefits-teamwork-business-3250.html

thebridgemaker.com/10-wonderful-gifts-that-give-us-hope/

thoughtcatalog.com/rachel-hodin/2013/10/35-famous-people-who-
were-painfully-rejected-before-making-it-big/

tinybuddha.com

zenhabits.net

About Katarina Gaborova

www.psychologistinthehague.com
Den Haag, Netherlands
Member of the Nederlands Instituut van Psychologen (NIP)

Over the years, Katarina has lived in various countries and has been exposed to many different cultures. This is one of the reasons why she decided to offer psychological support to the international community of The Hague in the Netherlands. Although the majority of her clients are international students, new immigrants and expats, she also deals with clients who need psychological support for every-day challenges.

Work experience

Educational psychologist at Australian schools where she designed social-skills training programs. 2006, Centacare, Melbourne, Australia.

Member of a team responsible for designing and producing psycho-educational materials in Slovakia to be used as a resource for families dealing with trauma. 2007, M.D. group s.r.o, Trencin, Slovakia.

Private practitioner as psychologist, in conjunction with a general practitioner at the H.S. Ramdin's Medical Centre. The Hague, Netherlands since 2008.

Educational background

Masters in Psychology (Child & Family Psychology), 2007, Australian Catholic University, Melbourne, Australia.

Post Graduate Diploma in Psychology, 2005, Swinburne University of Technology, Melbourne, Australia.

Bachelor of Arts (Psychology/Psychophysiology), 2004, Swinburne University of Technology, Melbourne, Australia.

Certified Professional NLP Practitioner and Certified Professional Life Coach, 2013, Scottsdale, Arizona, USA

Testimonials

"Katarina is an outside the box thinker, who makes things happen."
—Jennifer Glaese, Psychotherapist.

"One unique thing about Katarina is the compassion she brings into her work and her excellent listening skills. I met her when I had a serious depression. Her psychotherapy skills really helped me fight depression and concentrate on my studies. Thanks for the great work you are doing Katarina."
—Kehinde Okanlawon

"Katarina has been counselling international students from all over the world at our institute. She has shown great insight in the problems that international students may face when someone is in unfamiliar surroundings for an extended period. She was able to hand them the right coping tools through therapy, enabling our students to successfully finish their studies".
—Martin Blok, Dean of Students, and counsellor,
Institute of Social Studies of Erasmus University, Netherlands

"I truly enjoyed working with Katarina as she not only listens, but based on your personality and the circumstances and the life you live, She provides options and solutions that would be most suitable for you personally making each session with her into a conversation you would have with someone whom you trust to be on the lookout for what is the best for you."
—Anon

CPSIA information can be obtained
at www.ICGtesting.com
Printed in the USA
BVOW05s1458150817
492011BV00012B/15/P